The Liberal Arts Techie

The Liberal Arts Techie

How To Break Into Your First Startup Job

Austin Gunter

Introduction

Thanks for picking up this book. If you're taking the time to read it, I assume you're looking for ways you can become better in your career so you can get a better job, get paid more, and live a more exciting life. Startups are a great way to do all three.

Startups are looking to hire amazing people to join their ranks, and if you're reading this book, I assume that you're either fresh out of college with a liberal arts degree and looking to navigate the job market, which is increasingly dominated by tech companies.

Or, you're reading this book because you, just like me, got a liberal arts degree and found yourself in the job market and stalled, feeling underemployed, or have a voice gnawing at you that there is something better you could be doing with your time than sitting at a job that doesn't challenge you, is unfulfilling, and isn't making you a better human being.

My entire career has been in tech startup companies, and I can attest to the way they can change your life for the better. There are few working environments where you can go in every day and get paid to learn, to grow, and to be part of creating something brand new from scratch.

Startups give you the chance to experience the birth of a new business, and to be part of the growth and evolution of the company (and everyone in the company who contributes along the way) experiences.

Compared with working at a big corporation, startups are more fulfilling, more exciting, and there are more opportunities for you to grow within an organization that is, itself growing.

Getting hired at a startup is very doable, but a lot of the ways people were trained to interview by guidance counselors or by their parents are outdated (and sometimes just plain wrong) so folks miss out on an opportunity to join a company that could change their life.

I've put everything I know about getting hired at a startup company into this book. This comes from my personal experience interviewing at places like Google, Facebook, Box, Uber, and WP Engine. It also comes from lessons I've learned over the past several years coaching people on their resumes and how to interview.

This book is designed to familiarize you with how startup companies interview candidates so there are no surprises. And knowing how these companies hire will give you the confidence to kick ass at every step of the way.

There are also stories and lessons that are designed to challenge the way that you currently think about work, having a job, and getting a better one. One of my guiding beliefs is that when I am in a situation that I'm not satisfied with, it's because I need to think about things differently. Once I have changed my thinking, I always realize that I have an opportunity to do things just a bit differently, and that difference puts my life on a brand new track.

I want this book to help you shift your thinking, to recognize that there are new opportunities all around you, and give you the courage to take the first step towards a better life.

Austin W. Gunter
austin@austingunter.com

There's More?

As a thanks for picking up this book, I've put together a gift of additional resources for you.

I've interviewed at some of the hottest tech companies like Google, Facebook, and Uber, and coaching many people on how to get in the door and get hired at Silicon Valley startups.

If you want free access to my guides on how to thoroughly research the company you're interviewing for (in under an hour), and a huge list of specific questions you can ask during your job interviews be sure to sign up for my email list where I regularly publish about startups, life, and sometimes love.

Here is the link to sign up and get those resources for free:
www.austingunter.com/techie-gift

—Austin

1.

Everything You Know About Interviewing Is Probably Wrong

Just a few years ago, I was graduating with an English degree in the depths of the recession of 2008–2009. I had no job prospects, and no clue about how the whole getting a job thing worked. All I knew was that the job I had been promised my whole life after "getting good grades" and "graduating" wasn't anywhere to be found.

Nobody recruited me out of college. Nobody was accepting resumes, at least not from English majors.

I had lived inside the safe bubble of higher education, but now I was a college graduate completely unprepared to greet the real world around me and get a damn job.

College and my parents hadn't prepared me for what I needed to learn about finding work. The world had changed since they had been in the market. Companies had quit hiring people and training them up, planning for them to be employees for ten, twenty, thirty years. Companies were hiring people like puzzle pieces—people who fit into a role and could add value as soon as possible without having to wait 6–12 months for the person to be trained and able to contribute to the bottom line.

I spent the better part of that summer applying for jobs and not hearing back until I finally met the founder of a startup incubator at a networking event. Someone introduced us and told him I was looking for a job. He looked me up and down and then he said one thing that transformed my life and my career.

"Come to the incubator tomorrow. I'm sure we have something for you to do."

I said, "Ok," and asked for the address. He literally told me to Google it, which was a pain because it was hidden in the back of a bunch of warehouses. But I found it.

That was my first interview.

After driving around searching for the incubator, I walked in the door and did a day's worth of writing: 3 blog posts that were published on the site that evening. Then I showed up the next day and did some more work.

That was my second interview.

By the end of the week, he asked me to write a job description for myself and tell him how much I should get paid. I wrote the job description, but didn't ask for nearly enough money, and he hired me on the spot.

That was my final interview. I had a job.

It's important to stop and note that this first job didn't pay me very much at all. It was just enough to live on, but I was learning an incredible amount about the tech world, and about entrepreneurship, and about what it would take for me to establish my place in that exciting tech world.

This time involved a massive amount of learning for me, and that learning has propelled the last several years of my career forward, but at the time a lot of it sucked. I was confused about where my life was heading,

I didn't have a ton of money, and all of my early beliefs about work and life were being challenged.

I viewed the time as graduate school, except instead of having to stop working and take out loans, I was getting paid to learn and grow. I didn't have to leave the workforce to learn all these things, I was able to learn them on the job.

And meanwhile, I was building an incredible network, boosting my confidence, and exploring what my career could be by *actually doing the work* rather than reading about other people doing the work.

This job got my foot in the door of tech, and I wouldn't have been able to bridge the gap without it.

I tell you this because your first move into a new career may be a lateral one, or it may feel like a step backwards. It may feel like you're starting again from square one, but that's really what creating something brand new is. Starting fresh means starting from square one.

And once you build up a bit of momentum, very big things will start to happen.

Two and a half years later, I got hired at the hottest startup in Austin, Texas as the 12th employee. That job happened because I started doing freelance writing for the founder on their blog, and then after a few months I wrote another job description and got hired to do content marketing, social media support, and build the community.

Notice that I was a liberal arts major, but I took my core liberal arts skill, writing well, and leveraged it to get me in the door of tech companies.

Ask yourself, what is your core liberal arts skill, and how can you leverage it to get yourself in the door of the company you want to work for.

Amazing things will happen when you leverage the skills and training you DO have.

For example, a year later that company moved my liberal arts self from Austin to San Francisco.

By this point, I had already interviewed at Facebook (didn't get a job offer), and Google (got an offer, but turned it down), and the real world had shown me more how to get hired in this new economy than anything I'd learned at school or from a guidance counselor.

Guidance counselors will give you a cheesy aptitude test and then tell you to go to law school and be a lawyer, or that you should be a psychologist. Neither of those careers are things 90% of college students should consider. Most lawyers hate their jobs, and to become a psychologist takes a decade of further education, racks up a lot of debt, and doesn't pay very well. They will give you horrible resume advice that might have worked in the mid-80s, but has absolutely no place in the modern job market.

What I found in the real world was that the way I had been trained to think about work and getting jobs was completely wrong, particularly at early-stage startup companies where I wanted to work. At these startups, I found that there was a place for me if I did three things more or less right:

1. Hustle my way in the door and get myself noticed.
2. Demonstrate that I was a cultural fit for the company.
3. Deliver a lot of business value as quickly as possible so that the company wanted to keep me around.

Turns out that just like you, I had a lot I could offer to companies. I simply had to learn how to identify where my experience could add value to the business and then communicate it well. Once I did that, they would give me a shot to prove my worth.

Along the way, I've learned to not hold myself back because I think I don't have the right experience or qualifications. Turns out people are less concerned about previous experience and qualifications if you start doing great work from day one. Experience and qualifications are needed for some jobs, like being a surgeon or being a lawyer, but many startup jobs can be had if you're willing to hustle. I'm proof of this. I was just some clueless kid who got a really fluffy humanities degree and didn't know the first thing about business and I still made my way into startups.

In reality, nobody at a startup is qualified for what they are doing, including the founders. Everyone at a startup is learning and making it up as they go along, which is why it's the perfect place to get a job if you want to make a transition. You don't have to have proven qualifications, you have the chance to prove what you can do on the job, and everybody else is too busy trying to figure out what to do (just like you) that they aren't going to be looking over your shoulder to make sure you do things "the right way."

There is no right way when you're getting started. The right way is the way that gets results.

That lesson is the biggest thing that you can take away from this book. There is no "right way" to move ahead in your career. There is no one way to get ahead. The way to get ahead is to find one thing that you can work a bit harder on, or be a bit more comfortable with the ambiguity than every other person looking for a job. Find a bit of risk that you can take, and then take it. Learn from it, and then take the next one.

If you focus on hustle and stay determined to get results, you'll earn your stripes and your paycheck. This will not let you down.

You can do this, and I'm here to help.

No matter what your end goal is, you'll find that getting better at your career and your business makes you better at life. You learn how to think more critically, to work harder (and smarter), and how to be more humble along each step of the way, and all of that will translate into more money in your bank account and more freedom to spend your time how you want.

This book contains the strategies I've used to get jobs at high-growth startups based in Austin, Texas, Auckland, New Zealand, Boston, and San Francisco. It contains strategies I've learned interviewing candidates while at these companies. It contains tips from my friends who have hired (and fired) more people than they can count.

If you take this book to heart, the ideas in here can change your life.

And the first step is to understand how to disrupt the modern startup interview process.

2.

Understanding and Hacking the Modern Startup Interview Process

Most interview processes are things you want to skip over. The traditional interview process is designed to eliminate people who on paper don't seem qualified for a startup job. If, like me, you are starting from scratch (or starting with a humanities degree), then you may not look great on paper to a technology driven startup. Again, this has almost no bearing on your ability to do a killer job. You know it. I know it. But many hiring managers hire conservatively, looking for qualifications on paper and ignoring amazing candidates that are standing right in front of them.

In reality, the best jobs are filled via personal networks, and every startup job offer I've ever received has been a direct result of knowing someone at the company who referred me into the hiring manager where I could write my own job description or prove myself via actual work I could do.

Remember, *it doesn't matter what school you went to or what previous experience you have if you can demonstrate your ability to hustle and do great work right away. This means if you lack experience, you want to find a way to skip the "normal" hiring process.*

The most effective way to get hired at a startup is to hack the process. I'll walk you through the traditional hiring process so you can understand how it works, and then we'll cover how to hustle/hack the process and skip unnecessary steps and get yourself hired for a job where you can hustle and crush it.

The Resume Sorting Process

Let's understand the resume process so we can then figure out how to hack the process.

When there is a job to fill, someone at the organization, usually in HR or recruiting, posts a job description for an "Awesome Startup Role" and gathers a ton of resumes. They filter through the resumes, skimming each one for about 30 seconds to toss out the ones that are obviously a poor fit.

Don't get your feelings hurt, but for all the time you may labor over your resume, recruiters and hiring managers will spend a tiny amount of time looking at it. They're just skimming for things that check the "yep, qualified" or "nope, not qualified at all" box.

If you're going the traditional interview route, your resume needs to be written in such a way that your qualifications leap off the page and smack people over the head with a baseball bat. Even an average resume will mask an otherwise amazing candidate and can be the difference between someone getting an interview or not.

The Phone Screen

The people with the best resumes get a phone screen.

The phone screen is usually done by the recruiter or the HR person as well. They'll reach out to schedule a phone interview to ask a set of questions about the role.

This will be a 30 minute call, and they will come prepared with some questions that came from a brief conversation with the hiring manager. The questions are designed to elicit relevant experience for the job. The phone screen is a fantastic indicator of what they are looking for in the position. Pay close attention to these questions because similar ones will come up again in greater detail during later interviews. These questions are a massive clue to what they are hiring for, what their objectives are for the role, and how the role will be measured.

Additionally, on these calls, the recruiter may ask you to suggest some ways you would improve their product or marketing. If you're interviewing for a marketing role, be prepared to suggest a few strategies or tactics that the company may not be using yet. If it's a product role, you'll want to suggest a few ways to improve the product.

If you get asked these questions on a phone screen, but don't have answers, there's a good chance you won't get an in-house interview. Don't let that happen.

The First In-House Interview

The candidates who pass the phone screen are then brought in for longer interviews with the team. This will be a much more intense interview that lasts 2–4 hours, and for more advanced jobs, the interview can last an entire day and involve dinner with key team members.

In-house interviews evaluate a handful of different aspects of each candidate's qualifications, and will be broken up into stages with different people interviewing you for 30–60 minutes. Each interviewer will take a different angle and be sussing out different things such as your task-related qualifications and experience, your cultural fit on the team, and your overall excellence level.

You should pay close attention to the type of person who is interviewing you for the role to get a clue for what they are looking for. For example, a senior person in a similar role to what you're interviewing for is going to be asking a lot of task-related questions about your experience. They're going to evaluate whether you can do the job itself. There's also usually someone from the company with a completely different role that will be trying to get a sense of how you'll fit into the company culture. That person basically wants to figure out if they like you and they want to make sure your values are in line with the company values.

Startup companies are very intentional about their values, and will do work early in the life of the company to codify them. They're often written down on the walls somewhere, and usually on the careers page of the website. Take careful note of those to make sure they do line up with your personal values, but also so you can speak to questions that relate to those values during your interview.

Pay attention to how each person you interview with asks you various questions, because each of them is trying to determine a different part of your qualifications. The questions they ask will give you a clue about what they are trying to learn about you.

For example, when I interviewed at Uber, I spent 2 hours with the people on the team I would be working with, and then they sent in someone from a completely different department to determine if I was going to "raise the bar" of the company by joining. This person's job was literally to check me out from both a cultural perspective, but also from a raw talent perspective to see if I would be someone who would "raise the bar" at the company.

Now, startups are always chaotic and disordered to one degree or another. The earlier the company, the more likely the place is an outright shitshow, but don't let that phase you. Everything is still getting built, and inside of the chaos is where all the opportunity lies.

Also, some values that a company will espouse will be complete bullshit—as in, the company isn't living up to them. Always probe and ask your own questions to gauge how people feel about the company.

Asking good questions can reveal a company with a culture you don't want to be part of and can save you from a bad environment.

The Homework Assignment

It's increasingly common for companies to have candidates spend some time putting together a plan of action for the role, or performing a real-world task, in order to see their actual ability to execute on work. They do this to make sure they don't hire someone who can simply interview well.

If you're interviewing for a marketing role, the presentation will involve putting together a plan for an initiative like an event. The company wants to see how you manage a budget, track a marketing funnel from first contact to lead and to sales.

Some folks hate the homework assignment because it can look and feel like free consulting work that the company can extract from you simply because you want a job with them. I empathize with this, but the homework assignment has become a fact of life. What's more, it gives you a way to prove to the team that you're awesome by the quality of your work. If you are afraid you don't interview well, the homework assignment is your opportunity to prove yourself by actually doing work.

It is free work, but, remember how I did free work to get my first startup job?

I've found that doing free work for companies I wanted to work for was one of the most powerful ways I could get a job. You have to give value to get value, and I am very comfortable offering massive value for free if it gets me in the door at a company I want to join.

If you're trying to break into a new industry, one of the fastest ways to do this is free work because you get to learn what the work actually looks like and you can prove to a company what it's like to work with you.

For example, Uber's interview process involved 2 different Keynote presentations, a blog post, and an email newsletter. I spent about 60 hours prepping, but I viewed it as time well spent. I learned a lot going through the reps of those presentations, and I was also able to repurpose one deck for a different interview 2 weeks later where I got an offer and accepted.

You can also create your own job description with this presentation by showing the company things they hadn't thought of that bring value to the organization. That's literally how I got my first two startup jobs: I wrote job descriptions that suggested a ton of things I would do, and how we'd measure the results.

The more you take charge of your job, the more control you'll have over your career and the more impressive you'll be to the people you work with.

The Second In-House: Presenting your homework

If they like your homework assignment, the company will invite you back into the office to present it. If a startup has a distributed team, this interview will be over a Google Hangout. I once did this from my bedroom in San Francisco to a team in Auckland, New Zealand. The purpose of this interview is to see how a candidate presents in front of a team and talks about the plan in detail. How well you can speak to your plan is a great indicator of how well you understand what you've put together.

The team will ask questions designed to see how thoroughly you understand your presentation, and how you handle pressure. They're looking for how adaptable you are and how well you think on your feet. This can feel very high pressure, but I find it very calming to remember that you don't actually have to have all the answers. Ambiguity and uncertainty are incredibly common in startups, so saying "I don't know" is something you will grow very comfortable with. If you don't have an answer, you can say so, and ask a response question to understand more detail.

In fact, many interviewers intentionally keep asking harder and harder questions to see where the limit of your knowledge is and then to gauge how you handle a situation where you don't know the answer. Again, it's a startup and you will be faced with situations where you have no idea what to do, so you don't need to have all the answers, but you can score points by showing them how you would approach learning what you need to know in order to solve the problem.

For example, "I don't quite know how the digital promotion budget would look without digging into the cost-per-click of keywords. Can you tell me how you guys normally think about spending money on digital promotion?"

Responding this way is excellent because 1) you aren't getting flustered by a question, which demonstrates your confidence, and 2) by asking an intelligent question as a follow-up, you can learn more about how the company operates, and it gets the interviewers talking.

Responding to questions and following up with a question of your own is actually a strategy that forms a critical part of crushing startup interviews. The strategy is called String Theory.

Aside: String Theory

String Theory is where you respond to an interview question and then follow up with a question of your own. This technique is something I stole from the very excellent e-book *Kill The Interview*[1], written by a partner at one of the Big 4 accounting firms on how to interview for a job at those companies. And since you're

---

1   https://drive.google.com/file/d/0B9-wWAOtuXSBemdBM1d5WE1jMUU/view

investing in yourself by reading this book, I highly recommend you deepen your investment and read that one as well.

String Theory is based on the rule that whoever talks the most in the interview loses. If you're the only one who talks in an interview, you aren't going to get the job. If you're the only one who is talking, you aren't learning about the company, you aren't learning about the role and tailoring your responses to it, and you aren't developing a connection with the person interviewing you. None of those three things make it likely for you to get the job.

String theory doesn't mean you respond to every question with a question. If you do that all the time, you're being a pain in the ass and potentially coming across as defensive or combative.

Rather, you want to spend about 60 seconds answering the question asked of you (don't go over 60 seconds or you risk droning on—if they want more detailed answers, they will *always* ask). Once you're done answering, follow up with a question back to the interviewer that elicits more information about the company and the role.

Example:

>**Interviewer:** "Tell me about your startup experience."
>
>**You:** "Well, I've been working on small scrappy teams for a lot of my career, but a lot of my experience has been inside of larger organizations where I was able to learn the best practices, and map those to working on brand new initiatives with smaller teams. *What

sort of startup experience do the folks on your team have?"

Interviewer: "Well, not everyone has worked at startups. Some have and some haven't. We really value startup experience since we are starting one ourselves, but there's always a lot of benefit from the best practice learned at larger organizations."

You: "That's awesome to hear. *So when the team may lack some of that best practice experience, where do you go to fill in the gaps?"*

See how that works? Intelligent questions will get the interviewer talking about the company so you aren't the one talking the entire time, and you're learning more about the organization at the same time. Asking an intelligent question is a signal that you are a discerning candidate who knows what they are looking for and has a solid base of experience to draw from. This is a signal to the interviewer that you're a Top Performer.

What's more, the more they talk about the organization, the more you do actually learn about the company and what you're getting yourself into. This also gives you a sense for whether or not you'd actually want to work at the company. I'll get into why it matters for you to decide that you actually think working at the company would be fun later on. And the more you learn about the company via their answers, the better you're able to speak to things that resonate with them.

Note: The String Technique works wonders in social situations as well (e.g., first dates).

3.

Hacking the Interview Process

As we covered earlier, the reason you need to understand the interview process is so that you can *identify the steps that you want to skip*.

Remember all that talk in elementary school about not skipping steps and showing all your work? I always thought that was ridiculous and pedantic. If I could figure something out in my head, why do you want me to waste time showing my work? Turns out, skipping steps is what startups call "hacking" the process. It means you are able to find more efficient ways to get things done, which is key in startups since resources are so scarce. Skipping steps is a signal to the company that you can get more done with less, and that is exactly the type of person they want to hire.

The idea of hacking things in startups comes from computer hacker culture, which has had a massive cultural influence on startups. Hackers specialize in finding vulnerabilities, weaknesses, or inefficiencies in a system (it doesn't have to be computers), and then they exploit the weak point to their own ends. Hacking a system means you can make it do something you want it to do, but it wasn't necessarily intended to do.

The meta-concept to understand here is that just because a system (like the interview process) exists in a certain way, doesn't inherently mean the system is the most efficient way to get something done (like get hired). It just means that someone set the system up this way and it hasn't been sufficiently inefficient that people have wanted to stop what they're doing to go back and fix it.

What you need to remember is that every system was set up by some fallible human being, and is therefore subject to being questioned. In a startup, it's highly valuable to question an existing system in order to find a faster or more efficient method of getting shit done.

Hiring by sorting through resumes is, by definition, inefficient, and therefore is something you should look for ways to hack.

The reason we still use resumes is 1) it's a holdover from a previous era, and 2) it saves people time because you can sort through 100 candidates in half an hour on paper when meeting all 100 candidates in person would take weeks.

But again, resumes only reveal qualities you can put on paper, like what school you went to, and where you've worked in the past. As someone who went to a very average school, and doesn't have Google or Facebook on his resume, but who does well in startup companies because of things that you can't put on paper, like hustle and ability to learn and grow quickly, I can tell you that if all you went on was my resume, you'd miss a very good candidate.

You can be a super talented individual, but you may not have been able to spend $200,000 on your education to go to one of the Ivies, and in startups you absolutely don't have to.

Given how resumes are limited in their ability to show a company how awesome you are, you should look for other ways to get an interview rather than blindly sending in resumes.

How do you do this? You get introductions and referrals.

When I got my job at the second startup in Austin, it was because I had breakfast with the company's 5th employee. He was someone I barely knew, but I was on the hunt for a job and so I reached out for breakfast. We had met once before, talked and exchanged information. We didn't have a strong relationship or many personal connections, but that didn't stop me from inviting him out to breakfast before work one morning. I was looking for a job, and I wanted to know what he was working on, so I came prepared with questions about this new startup, and I also had a pitch for him: "I want to do more copywriting and content marketing for startup companies."

That conversation turned into me freelancing at the startup for several months. I started off writing blog posts for a few hundred bucks each. After a couple of months of blog posts, I told the founder I wanted to work there, helped write a job description, and he offered me the job.

Need another example?

One day around the same time, I was searching on Twitter for all the recruiters I could find in Austin, following them, and seeing which ones I could start conversations with. I found a recruiter at Google, followed him, started a conversation, and a few days later he submitted me for a job at Google where I got the offer.

How did I go from a Twitter conversation to a job offer at Google in a few days? I made a genuine connection with him and didn't talk about work at all at first.

On his Twitter profile, he said he was from Argentina, which is the home of yerba maté, a South American tea that I am a huge fan of.

When I struck up a conversation, I didn't talk about Google or getting a job, but I talked about yerba maté and how I had lived in Chile and visited Argentina when I was in college. Boom, we had a ton of things in common and could have a conversation.

If I had said right out of the gate, "OMG YOU WORK AT GOOGLE, CAN I HAVE A JOB WITH ALL THE FREE FOODS?", he would have blocked me on Twitter and had the locks changed at his house immediately. I wouldn't have been adding any value or trying to connect with him as a human being before trying to network.

Because we made a genuine connection based on a common interest, after a few back and forths, I was able to tell him I was also hunting for a job and he put my name into the system at Google. I got the interview and a job offer.

You can duplicate this sort of connection no matter what your network looks like, so don't give me any excuses. I didn't have a single connection to Google at the time, but I found something we were mutually interested in, yerba maté, and that was enough to spark a genuine connection and expand my network. It really is that simple.

As long as you are willing to make the effort to do some research and find out what people are interested in and how you can add value to them, you will have zero issues building your network. For more on how to make this work, you should read the blog post, *How to Connect with Busy People*[2] by Ramit Sethi, the baller behind **iwillteachyoutoberich.com**, which has a wealth of information about how to accelerate your career.

Using LinkedIn to Get Interviews

You can do this on LinkedIn incredibly easily as well. The following method will take a couple of weeks, but it will get you introductions to a number of companies that you'd love to work for.

A process for getting intros into a company you want to work for even if you don't have a network.

1. Make a spreadsheet of about 20 companies that you want to work for.

---

[2] www.iwillteachyoutoberich.com/blog/how-to-connect-with-busy-people/

2. Go to the company pages, select employees who work there, and make a list of employees who work in the department where you'd want to work: marketing, sales, etc. Add their names into one column of the spreadsheet, and the URL for their LinkedIn into the next column. You should be able to get a number of people in each department you'd like to work for.
3. Next, you do some research into their careers (based on their LinkedIn profiles) and figure out a bit about what they do. If they have blogs, you want to skim them. If they Tweet, you want to follow them on Twitter and see what they are interested in and what they talk about online. Make some notes of who they are and what they do in your spreadsheet.
4. Finally, you craft an individual email to each person asking to buy them coffee in order to learn more about the company. You're just asking for information, not asking for a job, or telling them you're looking. You're simply reaching out to learn more about their organization, company culture, their customers, and what their biggest challenges are.

Your goal is to interview them for 20–30 minutes over coffee or over video chat to learn about their company, and to make them like you. These informational conversations will do at least one of the following things.

1. You'll make a new friend and expand your network.
2. They won't have a job that's a good fit for you, but they will make an introduction to someone else you should take out for coffee.
3. They do have a job you're a good fit for, and they'll refer you to the recruiter, hacking part of the interview process.

If you don't have a network at all, this is how you start building one from scratch. Anybody can do this, but most people won't because they are afraid of being rejected while they are networking. The people who do take this step will accelerate their career in a very meaningful way.

But how do you network with busy people who are (ostensibly) more important and busier than you?

> **Aside: Add value in order to network with people busier than you**
>
> One of the people who has influenced me the most in my career is Ramit Sethi, the dude who owns the incredibly descriptive domain, **iwillteachyoutoberich.com**. Ramit is my bible about how to network properly with busy, high-value people who can change your life and your career.
>
> The secret, if there is one, is to put yourself in their shoes and rack your brain until you can empathize enough with *why on earth they would want to spend time with you*. It's obvious why you want to spend time with them. They are awesome, have their shit together, and can surely add a lot of value to your life. Most successful people have a lot of value that they can add to a lot of people's lives, but most successful people have a lack of time and an over-abundance of demands on their time.
>
> If you want to spend time with them, you have to figure out a way to add value to them. My strategy has been to do free work for people.
>
> I worked with a former IBM executive and high-profile business coach on a book she was writing in exchange for life-changing mentorship. When we met, I had no job but she agreed to let me buy her lunch and talk about my career.
>
> At lunch, I told her I wanted her coaching, couldn't pay, but I could write for her. She needed a book written and I knew how

to write, so we had a mutual exchange of value. I solved a huge problem for her, and in exchange I got a wealth of advice, guidance, and growth.

Everyone has a unique skill to offer that can add tons of value to busy, important people. That includes you. You have something amazing you can offer to people you network with, so spend some time thinking about how you can do this.

Here are a couple of amazing resources for you to check out. They are all Ramit resources, and if you're struggling to think of how you could add value to the folks you want to network with, the folks you want advice from, and the folks who can offer you life-changing mentorship, I suggest you dive into all of them.

- http://theartofcharm.com/podcast-episodes/ramit-sethi-the-real-truth-about-networking-and-success-episode-399/
- http://www.iwillteachyoutoberich.com/blog/ramits-definitive-guide-to-building-your-network-with-scripts/
- http://www.iwillteachyoutoberich.com/blog/video-what-the-pros-know-about-networking/

Ok, once you've hacked the process and gotten your foot in the door at a startup, what comes next?

4.

What Startups And Tech Companies Are Looking For

What all startups don't need to know about you

You can tell that most people don't know how to communicate the value they provide to an organization based on the generic crap they put on their resumes and LinkedIn profiles.

Take a look around LinkedIn and you'll see phrases about the person being a "dynamic problem solver" who has skills like the ability to "thrive in a fast-paced environment" and other completely meaningless statements.

Think about it. "Dynamic problem-solver" doesn't actually mean anything. Does it bring anything specific to mind when you read those words? No, it doesn't.

Being a dynamic problem solver and knowing how to thrive in a fast-paced environment are table stakes for joining a startup. In fact, that goes for any company that is adopting high tech—and every company is adopting high tech these days—so putting that on your resume is a bit like saying you know how to send an email.

There will be some crazy problems to solve at every step of the business. If you can't, or are unwilling to do that, then a startup may not be for you.

There is a right way to say that you're a dynamic problem-solver. It's by describing an event that required you to solve a problem, then to describe how you came up with the solution, and then to describe what the outcome was.

Here's a script that I've used that you can copy.

> **Interviewer:** "Tell us about a time you had to solve a big challenge for the company. How did you come up with your answer?"
>
> **Me:** "We were going to a regional conference where a number of our competitors would be attending, including GoDaddy, who were going to launch a competing product at the conference, using social media. Twitter, in particular, was going to be a huge promotion channel for them.
>
> "We wanted to run our own Twitter campaign that would drown them out, or at least compete with their launch to minimize it as much as possible.
>
> "I knew that our users still hated GoDaddy's misogynistic brand, so all we had to do was run a campaign using the keywords related to that event with messaging and branding that we knew they would like, and would allow us to take the spotlight from them.
>
> "To do that, we launched a customer-focused podcast the day of the event and gave away really well designed t-shirts celebrating the launch. We promoted the podcast and the shirts using the same keywords and hashtags that GoDaddy was using, and because the conference attendees engaged

more with our Tweets than GoDaddy's, Twitter automatically served more of our content than theirs.

"With a pretty minimal ad budget of a couple hundred bucks and some t-shirts, we were able to completely bury GoDaddy's competing product launch."

Interviewer: "That's pretty badass."

Me: "Right? It was a fun day."

Even if you don't have tech experience yet, you have a similar story that illustrates your hustle and ingenuity. Everyone has a story like that. If you aren't immediately thinking of one, pull out a sheet of paper and spend 10 minutes writing down things you've done at various jobs. Chances are you'll be surprised at all the cool work you've done along the way.

As you do this, keep in mind that the point isn't that you tell them a story about how you did something amazing at another tech company. The point is to tell them a story that shows them how you get shit done and think creatively. Your past performance will be indicative of future success, so mine your past for those stories and start telling them. You'll be surprised how well these stories work.

The three things that startups actually want to know about you.

Now that you are removing all the meaningless statements from your resume and your vocabulary, you'll need to know what goes in their place. Here are the top 3 things startups need to know about you.

1. You understand the company and the industry because you did your research.

2. You are ambitious and committed to personal and career growth, and you know that working at the startup aligns with your growth.
3. You have other companies that want to hire you, but you want to work for this one.

1. You understand the company and industry because you did your research.

There are very few things that blow away a startup interviewer more than having a candidate that is familiar with the market where the startup is operating. Familiarity with the market and with the customers means that you don't have to spend as much time ramping up when you join. You can make an immediate impact on the business.

Doing your research on the company means you know who some of their competitors are. It means you know who their customers are, and why their customers like to buy. It means you've spent some time watching their YouTube channel to see how they market to their customers. It means you've read news articles featuring the company. It means you have a sense of what their company culture is like from taking a look at their social media channels and digging around on their careers page.

Startup companies are very big on their outward brand and identity, and the more familiar you are with how they present themselves to the world, the better prepared you'll be for the interview.

> **Aside: how to do your research before the first in-house**
>
> Spend a while looking at the company's website and googling around for articles about them. You can learn an amazing amount about who their customers are, their company values, their products, and how they sell and market to their customers. This

is a critical step that should take you an hour or so, but not very many applicants will do this. There are always questions that come up in interviews that you can easily answer if you've taken a good look at their website.

Doing the research means you can both speak intelligently about how your skills and background will add value to the org, but also so you can ask clarifying questions about the company. A couple of good clarifying questions about their customers will really make you stand out.

What to Google

- Recent mentions of the company in the press/other blogs
- Research the product and the industry and competition
- Who uses the product? Small businesses? Large enterprises? Consumers?
- Why do they use the product? How does it make their lives easier/better?
- What product features are key to how they sell it?
- What direction is the industry heading?
- What is the philosophy of the company—what is the "big mission" for why they serve their customers, and how is this baked into their culture?

Read this as well: *8 Major Keys to Success and Getting Hired in the 21st Century*[3]

---

3   https://medium.com/the-mission/8-major-keys-to-success-getting-hired-in-the-21st-century-c6fc061fc30e#.tdi2jin47

2. You are ambitious and committed to personal and career growth, and you know that working at the startup aligns with your growth.

Startups don't want to hire people who are showing up at work for a paycheck. There's too much work to be done for you to be able to phone it in and make a meaningful impact, and you should know that going in. You work at a startup because it's a place where you have a huge opportunity to get better, and because you want a situation where your efforts will make a meaningful impact. You won't find a more committed, driven, inspiring group of people than are working in startups, and the energy is addicting. But make no mistake, it's a ton of hard work.

Jobs at startups aren't jobs. Startups are a cause where you go to learn a ridiculous amount in a very short period of time. They require commitment, and a willingness to grow and learn. The people who do best at a startup understand that by working there, they will align massive career growth with massive company growth. Startups hire people who can grow and learn as quickly as the company will need to grow in order to be successful.

How fast do you need to grow? Well, think about how quickly startups can grow. An early stage company can go from a few hundred customers to a few thousand customers in a year. That means the company can undergo a massive amount of growth and evolution in a short period of time.

Do you think the company can grow if its employees aren't?

No, it can't. Startups grow only as fast as their people do, so strap in for it.

3. You have other companies that want to hire you, but you want to work for this one.

Startups need to hire amazing people who can both add value quickly, but also have a high ceiling of growth. These are called A-Players. The reality about A-players is that they always have options about where they can go work, and they get to choose where they want to work. Smart startups know how to suss out whether a candidate is being mercenary rather than interviewing with the company because they are passionate about the company's mission. You need to both be in-demand, but also be choosing to work at the company. Nothing makes a hiring manager happier than hearing, *"This company is where I want to spend this stage of my career."*

What Startups Look For

Startups hire differently than larger companies, and while startup companies used to be the exception to the rule, as technology continues to transform the way businesses are run and how quickly they need to move, the qualities that startups look for in their employees will become much more in demand across all jobs.

In other words, the things startups look for will soon be the things most companies look for, and the lessons in this book will be more useful each year.

Startups are incredibly dynamic environments. They are full of uncertainty because the company is essentially having to discover a brand new business model. Startups exist to bring a new product to market, and this means a new sales process, a new type of customer support, a new way of marketing and positioning things, and a new way of building a product.

As you can imagine, this is very hard to do. It's not like a job at an established company where there is a process developed for everything.

At a startup, chances are good you'll get to create all the processes yourself. *After all, where do you think business processes come from in the first place?*

And startups are very fast-paced because they are usually not profitable yet, and are existing on investment from venture capitalists. They need to move fast so that they don't run out of money and go out of business.

Startups are also really tight-knit environments. Particularly for the first 20 employees, the relationships are very strong, and almost family-like. Everyone is working passionately, living and breathing the business, and (usually) having a lot of fun. A certain intimacy naturally develops that's hard to describe until you experience it yourself for the first time.

Startups hire people who can fit into that sort of environment, and that usually comes down to the following qualities.

1. A high level of flexibility and adaptability—because startups are constantly evolving, you need to be able to keep up with a high degree of change and uncertainty. It's not uncommon to get one set of orders from company leadership only to learn something new about your customers or the market and realize you need to change directions. People who are uncomfortable with this level of uncertainty simply aren't a great fit for startups.
2. Hustle—In a startup, everything must be earned. New customers have to be sold. Marketing has to be done on the cheap. There are no existing processes or "right way" to do things. In the midst of all this ambiguity all members of a startup need to hustle. Everyone does more work than their fair share. Everyone has to go out of their way to make something happen. The hustle is what you're demonstrating when you find ways around the traditional interview process. It's what you're demonstrating when you find a creative way to

add value to your mentors. The hustle is the sign of someone who sees obstacles and finds an innovative way to get around them.
3. Culture Fit—This is a fuzzy term. Culture is often a good way of saying, "we like this person and want to work with them." Culture fit means that if you get stuck with someone in an airport because of a flight delay you will have fun sitting at the bar with them. But culture fit also means that you make other people more productive.

Culture is made up of the way the company approaches building their product and connecting with their customers.

A great example is the culture of Apple. You can walk into an Apple retail store and feel their company culture. They have an intense focus on designing a refined user experience. There is nothing extraneous in the store. Just tables with products. Their retail store is designed to get you what you need as quickly as possible. Their phones are designed to get you what you need as quickly as possible. Both the retail experience and the iPhone experience emanates from their culture, and a great deal of work has gone into making both experiences so intuitive.

The startup you will interview at will have their own set of cultural values that should be evident in their products and their marketing.

Another way of describing culture is to say, "culture is a shared way of doing something with passion."[4]

The stronger the culture in a startup, the less corporate process needs to exist because the company can trust everyone to do the right thing according to the company culture and values. This means that when people are assessing you for cultural fit, they are looking to see if they can trust you as a member of the company tribe, as someone who can join

---

4   https://medium.com/@bchesky/dont-fuck-up-the-culture-597cde9ee9d4#.llmq32m1g

the ranks and do the right thing for the organization regardless of whether someone is watching or not.

Here's another great read on startup company culture[5].

Ok, now it's time to talk about the day of the interview.

---

[5] https://medium.com/@dunn/creating-culture-21a117803f80#.hl01lkb2v

5.

The Day of The Interview

It may seem obvious, but make sure you build in time beforehand to do the normal things you would do before any important meeting like finding parking, locating the office and going to the bathroom. You'll want to allow extra time for this because the last thing you want is to be stressed about being late (or actually late). The more you plan ahead, the more confident and prepared you'll feel. This will show up in your body. When you're in the interview, you want to be calm and comfortable. This is hard to do even when conditions are right, so make it as easy as possible by planning ahead.

How to dress

How to dress at a startup is really simple. Startups are incredibly casual, so you don't need to pull the suit out. In fact, if you wear a suit, it's pretty likely that they will think you don't know what you're doing because nobody at a startup ever dresses up that nicely except for the occasional wedding and funeral.

In 2010 I interviewed for a job at Facebook when they opened their

Austin office. Before I walked in the door, I asked the recruiter, "What do people dress like at the office? How should I dress for the interview?"

The recruiter explained that everyone dressed pretty casually, and to not worry about going too crazy. He even went so far as to say that sometimes people show up wearing suits to the interviews and it was usually awkward and those people aren't a good fit for the company. Nobody who works at a startup wants to wear a suit every day, so don't show up in one.

If you have questions, a good rule of thumb is to just ask the recruiter. You can always say, "What's the office culture like in terms of dress? I'm thinking about how I should prepare for the interview." They'll tell you how people in the office dress, and you can take it from there.

How Top Performers Think About Job Interviews

It's critical to mentally prepare yourself before you go into an interview, so let's think about how top performing candidates think about job interviews.

Picture one of those ridiculous high achievers who graduated from Harvard or Stanford, had internships at Google and Facebook, and can get a job anywhere. Now, you might not realize that someone like this also gets nervous about going into a job interview. As if their life experience or Ivy League degree somehow makes them immune to normal human emotions.

They're just like you. Where you went to school doesn't make them any more or less nervous when you're on the spot at a job interview or a first date.

The difference is their mindset and their goal when they take a job interview. Where most people are thinking, *"man, I hope I say the right things and get the job!"* a top performer is thinking, *"is this the company where I want to spend the next few years of my life?"*

They're not hoping to be chosen. They know that they want to spend their time working at an exciting place where they can learn and grow, so rather than worrying about "being picked" they are evaluating the company to see if it's a good place for them to invest their most precious asset: their time.

You're no different. The next few years of your life are just as valuable as anyone else's. And no matter how much you may believe you *need* a job right now (and perhaps you do need to find work), you should still place a higher value on getting hired than simply making a paycheck.

Just like being a dynamic problem solver is table stakes for joining a startup, getting paid decently is also table stakes. The company wants to pay you well so you're happy and can focus on doing amazing work. You don't have to trade exciting work for a paycheck. At startups, you get both.

When I interview at startup companies, I am asking a series of questions about the company. Things like, *"what can I learn here that I don't already know"* and *"how will this company grow me in my career and as a person"* and *"how can I make a massive impact on the company and its customers?"*

I want to know who I will be working for and reporting to in order to understand what I can learn from them.

I want to know who I'll be working alongside to see what they can teach me, and what I'll be able to teach them as well.

It's *my* career, and I want each stage of it to move me forward in what I bring to the table to each company, and how much money I am worth.

Thinking about your job in this manner puts you in a completely different mental and emotional state than *"gee, I hope they decide to hire me."*

If you're constantly thinking, *"gee, I hope they decide to hire me"* then you are going to come across as needy and desperate, and that's a sure sign that you aren't qualified for the job.

Contrast that with someone who is confident in the value they can provide to a company. They believe that they can contribute in an important way, whether through previous experience they can leverage or tons of hustle. The person who *knows* they can add value isn't interviewing *hoping* the company will pick them, they are interviewing hoping they find a company that is worthy of the next few years of their life.

They are asking, *"is this the best way I can spend my working hours for the foreseeable future?"* and this comes through as confidence that is incredibly attractive to a startup.

Job interviews are very similar to being on a date. If you're desperate for the other person to like you, you'll come across as incredibly unattractive.

But if you approach the date more casually, and ask questions to learn more about the person sitting across from you to see if you are a good match for each other, if you're confident in your ability to connect with people romantically, then it's much more likely that your date will see you as confident in who you are, where your life is going, and want to spend more time with you.

Startups, like serious relationships, are too much work and require too much of your heart and soul for you to "just get picked" by the first one that comes along.

When you interview, the company is getting to know you, but you're also getting to know the company. They should impress you just as much as you impress them. It's not enough for a company to extend you an offer. You also have to want to accept it.

The Interview

Let's cover a few of the basics of an in person interview.

- Plan to show up 15 minutes early—this demonstrates you can plan and work to a schedule.
- Bring a copy of your resume and something to take notes on if you like.
- Go to the bathroom before the interview.
- Look in the mirror, check your teeth, do some affirmations, and get ready to go crush it.

What to expect when you walk in the door

You'll greet the receptionist and tell them you're there for an interview. If it's a larger company, they will have an iPad where you sign in, have your photo taken, and get a name badge printed out. Larger tech companies will have you sign an Non-Disclosure Agreement (NDA) as well. This is a legal document that basically says you're not going to disclose any company secrets you may stumble across in the course of your interview. It's unlikely that you'll be exposed to anything that sensitive while you're there, so don't worry about it. Just sign the document because they won't let you interview if you don't.

From there, you'll be taken to a conference room where you'll be interviewed. They'll offer you something to drink. Accept their offer. You'll want something to sip on over the course of the interview.

They'll then tell you how the day is going to go, the order of the interview. From there, you're off.

Before everything else: Put yourself in the hiring manager's shoes

Chances are they don't know what they are doing anymore than you do. They aren't sure who they want to hire, and are feeling around in the dark. Nobody is born knowing how to hire. It takes time to learn.

They are hiring you to do some work for them. It's work that desperately needs to get done, and they're excited about the prospect of hiring someone awesome who will deliver on the work.

And if you know they might be taking a risk on you, then you can *voice* and *rebut* their objections before they make them.

For example, you can say, *"listen I know that it's not easy hiring someone new, and in this economy there are a ton of qualified candidates that you will interview, and you want to make sure you bring the best person onto the team. I've always heard that it's not the employee you hire that is the problem, it's the one that you don't fire soon enough. If I'm hired, I'll work very hard every day to live up to the opportunity you're giving me. I want to be an asset to this company and grow with the team."*

Saying something like that displays an incredible level of self-awareness and willingness to work harder than the next person, which puts you into an elite category.

What you want to accomplish in the interview

1. Ask questions to understand the job and the company very well
2. Convey that you are all 3 of the things that startups look for
3. Be memorable and create a genuine connection with everyone you meet with

How to tell the story of your career

One of the things you'll be asked to do in an interview is to "tell the interviewer about yourself." This isn't a question about your hobbies. This is a question about your career that needs to cover your qualifications for the job at hand. You need to be able to tell this story in about 60 seconds and hit the highlights of your career. This is a teaser that gets them excited about you as a candidate.

Tell a story that connects each stage of your career to the next one. Start at the beginning and touch on each job to cover what you learned there, how you grew, what you accomplished, and how your efforts helped the company grow. Tie your story into things that will be relevant to the job you are interviewing for. Every story you tell about yourself is an opportunity to "show not tell" that you have the right experience and are a good fit for the company. So, if you have a story you want to tell that doesn't directly connect with the work you're being hired to do, you shouldn't be telling it.

This is part of why it's so crucial to do your homework—review the responsibilities for the job description, understand the company and their market, before you walk into an interview. If you've done your research, you'll have a very good sense about how to present yourself as a perfect candidate.

It helps to plan stories about times in your work history that correspond to the job description. Have these stories ready, but don't over-rehearse them. At each interview you do, you'll re-use your stories and make them better as you learn how to interview.

Part of telling your story involves explaining why you left each job to take the next one. Each company should seem to naturally flow into the next so that it seems like you've had a plan and a focus all along.

This is usually not quite the reality because everyone's career takes detours, but you still need to have a story about how things fit together.

Here's a good example:

"After accomplishing [some impressive shit that relates to the

job you're interviewing for], and spending 2+ years as a designer at XYZ Corp, I was interested in a new challenge that involved more management of the creative process, so I joined ABC Corp where I had the opportunity to contribute to the rebranding of the company."

This tells a story of you being in control of your career rather than your career controlling you, and shows the hiring manager that you are intentional about making sure each job is a step up for you. This means if they offer you a job and you accept it, they are confident that you're making a conscious decision to join based on what you'll be able to learn and contribute to the company as opposed to accepting the first good job offer that comes your way. It also clearly communicates how you grew at each job, which means you're the type of person whose contributions to the company will grow over time.

In an interview, never say anything negative about anywhere you worked. Only morons say things like, *"I really hated my manager and didn't get along with a lot of my co-workers so I took a better job when it came along."*

If you have a bad boss, be gracious and focus on the things you learned and what was good about the job. Always focus on the positive aspects of each company. Find something you've learned or a way you've grown and share those stories in your interview. Keep it positive and keep it classy. The second you begin talking about how stupid your boss was, you may as well end the interview.

Have more than just one story

Good interviewers will recognize if you have rehearsed your story a bit too well, and as soon as you're finished talking, they'll ask you a follow-up question to give another example from your career. This is designed to weed out the people who may simply be really good at interviewing, but are all talk and no execution.

Another technique that smart interviewers will use is called "behavioral interviewing" where they don't ask you how you *would* accomplish something in your new job, but how you *have* accomplished that same thing at a previous role. They're trying to use your past performance as a way to gauge your future performance.

To make sure you are ready for either question, be prepared to explain the process that you went through to accomplish various projects at various times in your career. The more detail you can explain about how you plan things out, what you plan out, how you measure your results, how you schedule your time, who you reported to and what information they wanted or didn't want, the clearer picture you'll paint for the hiring manager about how awesome you are.

In particular, the more clearly you can articulate a strong process to them, and the more you can apply the principles of what made your efforts successful in one situation also successful in another, the more confident they will be that you're highly competent at what you do.

Getting Culture Fit

You're not just looking for a good career move, you're also looking for a great culture fit. This means that you fit with the people in the company, and the company fits with you as well.

You want to impress your new company with how awesome you are, but you also want to make sure they hire you for your true personality, not an act you're putting on. The last thing you want is to end up in a company where you don't quite fit in because you aren't a culture fit but nobody realized that in the interview process because you weren't being yourself.

This happened to me in one of my first jobs. I got hired at a company that didn't do a great job of checking for culture fit, and I ended up having very little in common with most of the people I was working with, which made it incredibly hard to come to work every day. I was miserable every day going into work, and hated being in the office. The company pretty much felt the same way about me. Nobody should have to go spend 8+ hours a day, five days a week with people that they don't get along with very well. Life is too short for that.

The best way to avoid ending up at the wrong company, and ensure you end up at the right one is to actually spend some time thinking through what your values are personally and professionally, and then be able to speak to those in the interview.

It's important to be formal, but to still be yourself in the interview. This can be hard because interviews are this weird artificial situation where you're trying to come across as both likeable and awesome to this person who decides if you get a job or not. However, part of what your interviewer is looking for is a sense of whether they think they'll get along with you, so hiding your personality altogether isn't helpful.

Now, this doesn't mean you should be buddy-buddy with your boss. It's still a working relationship. A better way to do this is to touch on your values and your character by telling a story about how you've acted in accordance with the company values, which are usually plastered all across the Careers page of their website, and often on the walls of the office as well.

How to end an interview

As the interview wraps up, it's important to do 3 things. First, summarize the experience that makes you a killer fit for the job. Second, emphasize that you're excited about the prospect of joining their team and culture. Third, ask what the next steps are in the process; the following script will work wonders.

> "I want to thank you for your time. Based on our conversation, I'm excited about the opportunity to learn more about the team at the next stage in the process, and from what I can tell, I think I'd be a good fit because of my experience in A, my skills in B, and the fact that I really resonate with your cultural values of C. I'm excited to take the next step in the process. What happens from here?"

Use the above to tie a bow around who you are as a candidate and to illustrate that you're a good fit, and to express your enthusiasm for the role. They want to hire someone who wants the job, so remember to tell them that you do.

Is it OK to say you're interviewing elsewhere?

It's absolutely OK to tell people that you are interviewing with a few other companies if you are. Top performers who are seriously looking for a new gig are almost always interviewing multiple places and the hiring manager is aware of this. When you confirm that you are interviewing elsewhere, this lets them know you're in-demand, and if they decide they like you, they'll move faster if you're in talks with other companies and may have offers coming.

Here is how you tell folks that you are interviewing elsewhere. Wait until the end of the interview, and as you are closing out with the script above, you can add the following:

> "I'm in the process of interviewing at a handful of places to find my next opportunity. Things are good at my current gig, and there's no rush for me to leave, but I am actively talking to a few organizations and I want to be transparent."

I know that sounds simple. That's because it is, and it works. You don't need to overthink this, and you know why?

Let's say you're that Harvard graduate who has spent the last 4 years working at Google and you're interviewing for this job. That person doesn't have to worry a bit about leaving their current gig because they're killing it, and they surely do have offers on the table from other companies because they are awesome at what they do. That's the type of person that a startup wants to hire.

Top performers are already doing well where they are, and will do well where they are headed. Top performers don't have to make a big explanation that they are interviewing anywhere else because *of course they are*. They have options! And because they have options they have the luxury of waiting for the right company, and they can tell the interviewer that.

This flips the script and makes the interviewer want to chase you a bit. Interviewing new candidates for a role sucks. It's a pain in the ass and takes up a LOT of time to interview 10–20 candidates to find the best fit. The hiring manager wants to find the most awesome person they can on their team, and the person with the most options is usually the most awesome candidate. Hiring managers will actually chase candidates like this, offering them more money, perks, and the like. You want to be this person.

6.

What Are The Next Steps In The Hiring Process?

Make sure you have a way to get in touch with them afterwards. If to this point you've been communicating through their career@company email address, you'll want to make sure that before they leave the room you get the contact information of everyone who interviews you. Ask for a business card or an email address if you have to. You want to send brief thank you's to all of them within 24 hours of your interview.

You would be amazed how few people send thank you emails after an interview. By not sending this email, they miss a critical opportunity to stand out from the rest of the applicants. Sending a really good follow-up email is your chance to reinforce the strong impression that you left in your interview.

The format for this email is simple. First, thank them for their time. Second, say you're really excited or energized by the opportunity to join the company and *"have an impact on the industry."* Third, revisit the strongest moments in the interview by saying, *"Based on my experience with X and Y, I'm confident that I'll be able to make a big impact at the company and help you all achieve the goals you have."*

How to follow-up with emails throughout the process

One of the most crucial parts of getting a job happens after the interview is over. It's what happens as you're anxiously waiting to hear back from the company to come in for the next interview, or waiting for them to make you a job offer.

In 2014, I was interviewing at two companies, so I had my first choice and my second choice. As it seems to always happen, my second choice gave me an offer right away, but my first choice, the company I really really wanted to work for delayed for a good week to give me an offer. I kept having to hold the other company off and say that I needed more time before I could accept their offer.

Meanwhile, I needed to keep sending my first choice company emails to make sure they didn't forget about me and to keep nudging the process forward.

When you haven't heard back from the company in a week or so, it's very appropriate to send them an email to bring the hiring decision back to the forefront of their mind. Remember, they're busy with a million things at the office, and sometimes getting someone into the office can take a backseat.

You can always send an email that says something like this:

Hey [Hiring Manager],

I wanted to send you a quick note. Please let me know what else you may need from me to continue the hiring process.

Looking forward to talking more soon,

—Austin

7.

Wrapping Up

Awesome.

If you've made it this far, I'm stoked that you've made this investment in your career and in your future.

I'd like to revisit my career journey because it sums up why I so strongly believe getting the next leg up in your career can transform your life.

When I hit the job market in 2009, I had zero practical experience. Nothing on paper made me desirable on the job market other than the ability to write. I didn't understand business at all, had no concept of what tech startups were like, and didn't know the first thing about navigating the job market.

My parents were losing their minds a bit because it looked like I was spinning my wheels for months, looking for jobs but never getting hired. My dad was starting to put pressure on me to get a temporary, but crappy retail job just so I would "have a job."

But I had a hunch that would be a horrible idea. I believed that whatever job I got out of school would create a direction in my life, and that direction would gain inertia, and that "temporary" retail job might get comfortable and I might end up staying there for years only to look back and wonder what would have happened if I had held out a little bit longer for a job that had more upside, and would create opportunities for me to grow.

I listened to that voice, and held out until I found the first tech startup that would take a risk on me. And then I found the second tech startup that would take a risk on me. And then suddenly that startup had moved me from Austin to San Francisco, and was putting me in direct contact with some of the most intelligent, thoughtful, generous people in the world.

And then the next startup was based in New Zealand and started flying me back and forth between New Zealand and Toronto, giving me an incredible international perspective and giving me the opportunity to work with some incredibly talented folks who taught me a tremendous amount about business and about myself.

In the process, I've made some great friends. I've grown as a person. I've made more money than I could have imagined as a college graduate, and there is so much more to come.

The same is possible for you.

There are opportunities awaiting you that you can't imagine right now. Ways you'll evolve, people you'll meet, places you'll get to see. All you need to do is take that first step. Take a small risk on yourself. Step out of your comfort zone and seize an opportunity to upgrade your career.

You deserve to take the risk on yourself. And you deserve to be happy.

I believe in you.

And if you want to chat more about this, send me an email: **austin@austingunter.com**. I'll look forward to hearing your story.

Hope this helps.

—Austin Gunter

Still Want More?

As a thanks for picking up this book, I've put together a gift of additional resources for you.

I've interviewed at some of the hottest tech companies like Google, Facebook, and Uber, and coaching many people on how to get in the door and get hired at Silicon Valley startups.

If you want free access to my guides on how to thoroughly research the company you're interviewing for (in under an hour), and a huge list of specific questions you can ask during your job interviews be sure to sign up for my email list where I regularly publish about startups, life, and sometimes love.

Here is the link to sign up and get those resources for free:
www.austingunter.com/techie-gift

—Austin

Acknowledgements

A big thanks to the following folks for reviewing drafts of this, doing free work, and offering encouragement on this little project:

Chris Wilson, Zzane Guajardo, Benjamin Mikiten, Lauren Gunter Mikiten, Jason Evanish, Bryan Tublin, Anton Commissaris, Tyler Hayes, Brad Hart.

www.ingramcontent.com/pod-product-compliance
Lightning Source LLC
Chambersburg PA
CBHW070401190526
45169CB00003B/1057